Mastering the Forex Market

MASTERING THE FOREX MARKET

A Comprehensive Beginner's Course for Financial Success

BY
FRANK ONI

CONTENT

Introduction:

Welcome to "Mastering the Forex Market: A Comprehensive Beginner's Course for Financial Success." In this book, we embark on an exciting journey into the world of Forex trading, where the global currency market presents endless opportunities for financial growth and independence. Whether you're a complete novice with no prior experience in trading or an aspiring trader seeking to enhance your skills, this comprehensive beginner's course is designed to equip you with the knowledge, strategies, and mindset needed to navigate the Forex market with confidence and success.

Through a step-by-step approach, we will delve into the fundamental concepts of Forex trading, demystifying complex terms and strategies to provide you with a solid foundation. From understanding currency pairs and market dynamics to exploring technical analysis tools and risk management techniques, each chapter will build upon the previous one, empowering you to make informed trading decisions.

Beyond the technical aspects, we will also delve into the psychological aspects of trading, exploring the importance of discipline, emotional control, and developing a resilient mindset. By addressing the psychological challenges that traders often face, we aim to help you cultivate the psychological intelligence necessary to thrive in the dynamic Forex market.

Throughout this book, you will find practical examples, real-life case studies, and actionable tips to reinforce your learning and guide you in developing your personalized trading plan. Remember, mastering the Forex market is a continuous journey of learning and adaptation, and this book serves as your compass, pointing you in the right direction.

So, whether your goal is to generate supplemental income, achieve financial freedom, or simply gain a deeper understanding of the Forex market, "Mastering the Forex Market: A Comprehensive Beginner's Course for Financial Success" is your roadmap to unlocking the potential of currency trading and embarking on a path to financial prosperity.

Get ready to immerse yourself in the world of Forex trading and embark on a transformative journey that will forever change your approach to the financial markets.

Let's get started!

Introduction to Forex Trading:

What is Forex?

Forex, or foreign exchange, is the global market where currencies are traded. It is the largest and most liquid financial market, where participants buy and sell different currencies with the aim of making a profit from changes in exchange rates. Forex trading involves speculating on the value of one currency relative to another and can be done through various means, including online platforms provided by brokers. It's important to note that forex trading carries risks and requires knowledge and understanding of the market.

Why trade Forex?

There are several reasons why people trade Forex:

Potential for profit: Forex trading offers the opportunity to make profits by speculating on the movements of currency exchange rates. Since currencies fluctuate in value relative to one another, traders can take advantage of these price movements to generate profits.

High liquidity: The Forex market is the largest financial market in the world, with high liquidity. This means that traders can enter and exit positions quickly and at a desired price, even when dealing with large trading volumes. This liquidity ensures that traders can execute trades without significant price disruptions.

Accessibility: Forex trading is accessible to a wide range of participants. The market operates 24 hours a day, five days a week, allowing traders to engage in trading at their convenience. Online platforms provided by brokers make it easy for individuals to access the market and trade from anywhere in the world.

Leverage: Forex trading offers the option to use leverage, which allows traders to control larger positions with a smaller amount of capital. This leverage amplifies both profits and losses, providing the potential for higher returns. However, it's important to use leverage judiciously and understand the associated risks.

Diversification: Forex trading provides an opportunity to diversify investment portfolios. By including Forex in a portfolio, traders can spread risk across different asset classes, such as currencies, stocks, and bonds. Diversification can help mitigate risk and potentially enhance overall returns.

Hedging: Forex trading allows businesses and investors to hedge against currency risks. For example, companies involved in international trade can use Forex to protect themselves from adverse currency movements that may impact their profits. Hedging can provide a level of stability and mitigate potential losses.

Educational opportunities: Forex trading provides a learning opportunity for individuals interested in financial markets. Traders can develop skills in technical and fundamental analysis, risk management, and decision-making. The knowledge gained from Forex trading can be valuable for personal and professional growth in the financial industry.

Overview of the Forex market participants.

The Forex market consists of a wide range of participants, each with their own motivations and objectives. Here is an overview of the main participants in the Forex market:

Commercial and Investment Banks: Banks are the largest players in the

Forex market. They facilitate currency transactions for their clients, including corporations, governments, and other financial institutions. Banks also engage in speculative trading to profit from currency fluctuations and manage their own positions.

Corporations: Companies engaged in international trade participate in the Forex market to exchange currencies for conducting business operations. They may also use Forex to hedge against currency risks, ensuring that they can protect their profits from adverse exchange rate movements.

Central Banks: Central banks play a significant role in the Forex market. They implement monetary policies and interventions to stabilize their domestic currency and influence exchange rates. Central banks also engage in Forex trading to manage foreign exchange reserves and promote economic stability.

Institutional Investors: Hedge funds, pension funds, and other large institutional investors participate in the Forex market. They trade currencies as part of their investment strategies, seeking opportunities to generate returns and manage portfolio risks.

Retail Traders: Individual traders, also known as retail traders, are a growing segment of the Forex market. These traders engage in Forex trading for personal investment purposes. Retail traders typically trade through online platforms provided by Forex brokers.

Brokers and Market Makers: Forex brokers act as intermediaries between retail traders and the market. They provide access to the Forex market and facilitate the execution of trades. Market makers are a type of broker that create a market for traders by offering bid and ask prices.

Speculators: Speculators are traders who aim to profit from short-term price movements in currency pairs. They often use technical and fundamental analysis to identify trading opportunities. Speculators include professional traders, individual retail traders, and algorithmic trading systems.

Government and Sovereign Wealth Funds: Governments and sovereign wealth funds engage in Forex trading to manage foreign exchange reserves, diversify investments, and support economic policies. Their trading activities can have a significant impact on exchange rates.

Basic terminology: currency pairs, bid/ask price, spread, pips, lots, leverage, margin and equity.

Here are some basic terminologies commonly used in Forex trading:

Currency Pairs: Currency pairs represent the exchange rate between two currencies. They consist of a base currency and a quote currency. For example, in the currency pair EUR/USD, the Euro (EUR) is the base currency, and the U.S. Dollar (USD) is the quote currency. Currency pairs are quoted as the amount of quote currency required to buy one unit of the base currency.

Here's an example of a currency pair;

GBPUSDc

Bid/Ask Price: The bid price is the price at which the market is willing to buy a currency pair, and it is the price at which traders can sell the base currency. The ask price, also known as the offer price, is the price at which the market is willing to sell a currency pair, and it is the price at which traders can buy the base currency.

Here's an example of Bid/Ask price;

Spread: The spread refers to the difference between the bid and ask prices of a currency pair. It represents the cost of executing a trade. Brokers make their profit from the spread. A narrower spread indicates higher liquidity, while a wider spread implies lower liquidity or increased market volatility.

Pips: A pip is the smallest unit of measurement in the Forex market, and it represents the fourth decimal place in most currency pairs. It stands for "percentage in point" or "price interest point." For currency pairs with the Japanese Yen as the quote currency, a pip is represented by the second decimal place. Pips are used to measure price movements and determine profits or losses.

Lots: A lot is the standardized unit of trading size in Forex. It represents the volume or quantity of a trade. There are different lot sizes:
Standard Lot: A standard lot is equal to 100,000 units of the base currency.
Mini Lot: A mini lot is equal to 10,000 units of the base currency.
Micro Lot: A micro lot is equal to 1,000 units of the base currency.
Lot sizes allow traders to control their exposure to the market. For example, trading one standard lot of a currency pair means trading 100,000 units of the base currency.

Leverage: Leverage allows traders to control larger positions with a smaller amount of capital. It is a loan provided by the broker to amplify potential returns. Leverage is expressed as a ratio, such as 1:50 or 1:200. For example, with a 1:100 leverage ratio, a trader can control a position worth $10,000 by depositing only $100 as margin.

Margin: Margin refers to the collateral required by a broker to open and maintain positions. It is a percentage of the total trade value and is based on the leverage ratio. Margin requirements vary among brokers and currency pairs. Margin allows traders to magnify their potential profits or losses.

Equity: Equity represents the current value of a trader's account, taking into account open positions and unrealized profits or losses. It is calculated as the account balance plus or minus any floating profits or losses. Equity changes as trades are closed or as the market value of open positions fluctuates.

Here's an example of equity;

Balance:	164.65
Equity:	164.65
Margin:	0.00
Free margin:	164.65
Margin level (%):	0.00

Market Structure and Mechanics:

Understanding currency pairs and their notation.

Currency pairs are the foundation of Forex trading, and understanding their notation is essential. Here's an explanation of how currency pairs are denoted:

 A currency pair consists of two currencies, with the first currency being the base currency and the second currency being the quote currency.

The notation used to represent currency pairs follows a standardized format. For example, let's consider the currency pair EUR/USD:

EUR is the base currency, which represents the Euro.

USD is the quote currency, which represents the U.S. Dollar.

Here's an example of the base and quote currencies that makes a pair;

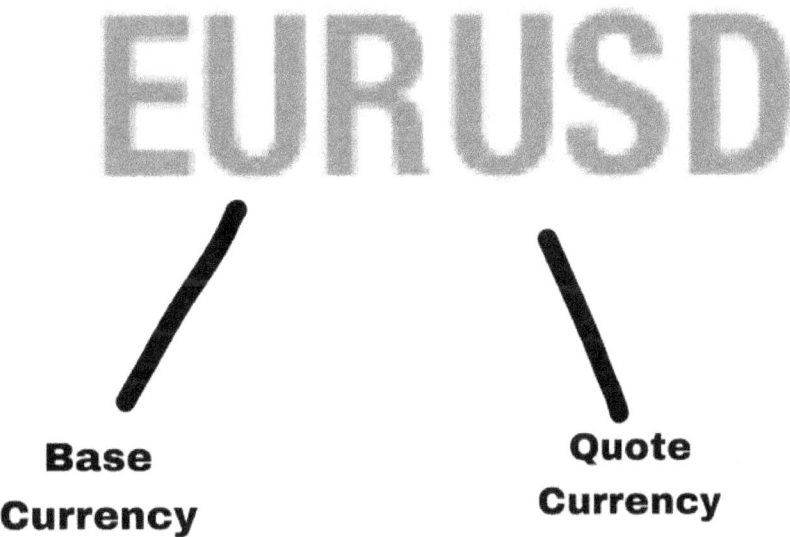

The base currency is the currency you are buying or selling, while the quote currency is the currency you are using to make the transaction.
In the Forex market, currency pairs are quoted with a bid price and an ask price. The bid price is the price at which the market is willing to buy the base currency, and the ask price is the price at which the market is willing to sell the base currency.

The currency pair notation indicates the amount of quote currency required to buy one unit of the base currency. Using EUR/USD as an example, if the current exchange rate is 1.2000, it means that 1 Euro is equivalent to 1.2000

U.S. Dollars.

In addition to major currency pairs like EUR/USD, there are also minor currency pairs (crosses) and exotic currency pairs. Minor currency pairs consist of major currencies other than the U.S. Dollar, such as GBP/JPY (British Pound/Japanese Yen). Exotic currency pairs involve one major currency and one currency from an emerging or smaller economy, like USD/ZAR (U.S. Dollar/South African Rand).

Currency pair notations are standardized across the Forex market, allowing traders and investors worldwide to identify and trade different currency pairs using the same conventions.

Major, minor, and exotic currency pairs.

Currency pairs in the Forex market can be categorized into three main groups: major pairs, minor pairs (also known as crosses), and exotic pairs. Here's an overview of each category:

Major Currency Pairs:
Major currency pairs are the most actively traded pairs in the Forex market and involve the world's most powerful economies. They include the U.S. Dollar (USD) paired with other major currencies. The major currency pairs are:

EUR/USD: Euro/US Dollar
USD/JPY: US Dollar/Japanese Yen
GBP/USD: British Pound/US Dollar
USD/CHF: US Dollar/Swiss Franc
USD/CAD: US Dollar/Canadian Dollar
AUD/USD: Australian Dollar/US Dollar
NZD/USD: New Zealand Dollar/US Dollar
These pairs often have high liquidity, tight spreads, and are influenced by major economic and geopolitical events. Major currency pairs are popular among traders due to their trading volume and availability of information.

Minor Currency Pairs (Crosses):

Minor currency pairs, also known as crosses, do not involve the U.S. Dollar as the base or quote currency. They represent currency pairs from major economies other than the U.S. The minor currency pairs are formed by pairing major currencies against each other. Some examples of minor pairs include:

EUR/GBP: Euro/British Pound
EUR/JPY: Euro/Japanese Yen
GBP/JPY: British Pound/Japanese Yen
AUD/CAD: Australian Dollar/Canadian Dollar
NZD/JPY: New Zealand Dollar/Japanese Yen
Minor currency pairs typically have lower trading volumes and wider spreads compared to major pairs. They can offer trading opportunities based on the specific dynamics of the respective economies.

Exotic Currency Pairs:

Exotic currency pairs involve one major currency paired with a currency from an emerging or less frequently traded economy. These pairs are less liquid and have wider spreads compared to major and minor pairs. Exotic currency pairs include:

USD/MXN: US Dollar/Mexican Peso
USD/TRY: US Dollar/Turkish Lira
USD/ZAR: US Dollar/South African Rand
EUR/TRY: Euro/Turkish Lira
GBP/TRY: British Pound/Turkish Lira
Exotic pairs can be more volatile and subject to higher risks due to the economic and political factors affecting the countries involved. Traders often require specialized knowledge and experience to trade exotic currency pairs effectively.

Understanding the distinctions between major, minor, and exotic currency pairs can help traders identify different trading opportunities based on their preferences, risk tolerance, and market conditions.

Introduction to market sessions and their characteristics.

The Forex market operates 24 hours a day, five days a week, excluding weekends. The market sessions refer to specific time periods during which trading activity is concentrated in particular regions of the world. Here's an introduction to the main Forex market sessions and their characteristics:

Asian Session:
The Asian session begins with the opening of the Tokyo market at 7:00 AM (GMT). This session is known for relatively lower trading volume and volatility compared to other sessions. The major financial centers active during this session include Tokyo, Singapore, and Hong Kong. Currency pairs involving the Japanese Yen, such as USD/JPY, tend to see increased activity during the Asian session.

European Session:
The European session starts with the opening of the London market at 7:00 AM (GMT). London is considered the financial hub of the Forex market. This session sees significant trading volume and liquidity, making it a favorable time for trading major currency pairs involving the Euro (EUR), British Pound (GBP), and Swiss Franc (CHF). Economic news releases from the Eurozone and the UK often generate market volatility during this session.

North American Session:
The North American session begins with the opening of the New York market at 12:00 PM (GMT). This session overlaps with the end of the European session, leading to increased trading volume and volatility. The major financial centers active during this session include New York and Toronto. Currency pairs involving the U.S. Dollar (USD), such as EUR/USD and USD/ JPY, experience high trading activity. Economic data releases from the United States and Canada can impact market movements.

Pacific Session:
The Pacific session, also known as the late Asian session, includes trading activity from Wellington (New Zealand) and Sydney (Australia). This session overlaps with the end of the North American session. Although it is relatively

quieter compared to the other sessions, currency pairs involving the Australian Dollar (AUD) and New Zealand Dollar (NZD), such as AUD/USD and NZD/USD, may see increased volatility during this time.

Here's an example of the trading session;

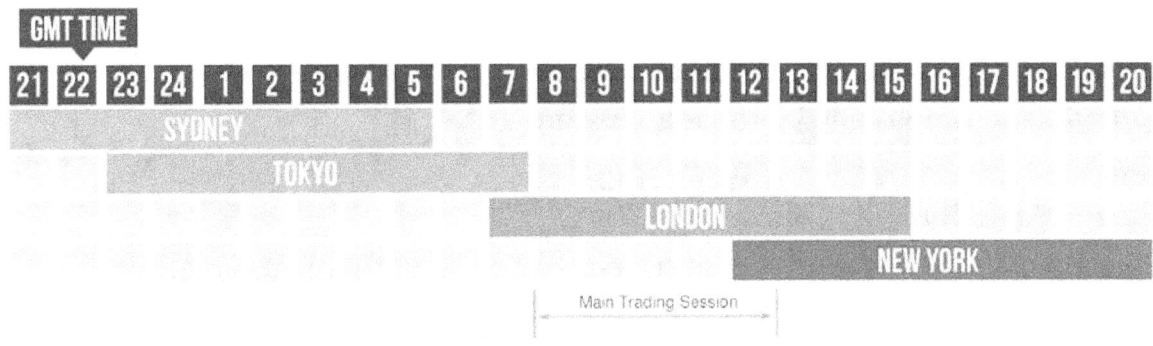

It's important to note that while each session has its own characteristics, the Forex market is technically open 24 hours a day due to the overlapping sessions. During periods of overlap, trading activity and liquidity tend to be higher, offering increased opportunities for traders.

Introduction to market liquidity and volatility.

Market liquidity and volatility are two important concepts in the Forex market that impact trading conditions and opportunities. Here's an introduction to both:

Market Liquidity:
Market liquidity refers to the ease with which an asset, such as a currency pair, can be bought or sold without causing significant price movements. In a liquid market, there is a high volume of trading activity, tight bid-ask spreads, and minimal slippage (the difference between the expected price and the executed price).

Liquidity is influenced by various factors, including the number of active participants, the depth of the market (the availability of buy and sell orders), and the trading volume. Major currency pairs, which involve widely traded currencies like the U.S. Dollar and Euro, tend to have high liquidity.

High liquidity is advantageous for traders as it allows for quick execution of trades, narrow spreads, and lower transaction costs. It also ensures that large positions can be entered or exited without significantly impacting prices. However, during periods of low liquidity, such as weekends or certain market sessions, trading conditions may be less favorable, with wider spreads and potentially increased slippage.

Market Volatility:

Market volatility refers to the degree of price fluctuations and market instability. It represents the speed and magnitude of price movements in a given market. Volatility can be influenced by various factors, including economic indicators, geopolitical events, central bank announcements, and market sentiment.

High volatility can present both opportunities and risks for traders. It creates potential for significant price swings, allowing traders to capitalize on short-term price movements. Volatile markets often provide increased trading opportunities and the potential for higher profits.

On the other hand, high volatility also entails increased risk. Prices can move rapidly and unpredictably, leading to potential losses if trades are not managed effectively. Traders need to be cautious during periods of heightened volatility and may employ risk management strategies, such as setting appropriate stop-loss orders and position sizing, to mitigate potential risks.

Low volatility, on the other hand, implies smaller price movements and a relatively stable market environment. During periods of low volatility, trading conditions may be calmer, with narrower price ranges. Traders may need to adjust their strategies to suit low volatility environments, such as employing range-trading or mean-reversion strategies.

Fundamental Analysis:

Fundamental analysis is a method used to evaluate the intrinsic value of a financial asset, such as stocks, bonds, or commodities. It involves analyzing various factors that can influence the underlying value of the asset, such as the overall economy, industry conditions, company financials, management quality, and competitive positioning.

Here are some key aspects of fundamental analysis:
Economic Analysis: Evaluating macroeconomic factors like GDP growth, interest rates, inflation, employment data, and fiscal policies to understand the overall economic environment and its potential impact on the asset.

Industry Analysis: Assessing the specific industry or sector in which the asset operates, considering factors like competition, market trends, regulatory environment, technological advancements, and barriers to entry.

Company Analysis: Examining the financial statements of a company, including balance sheets, income statements, and cash flow statements, to assess its financial health, profitability, debt levels, and growth prospects. Additionally, analyzing qualitative factors like the company's business model, management team, competitive advantages, and corporate governance.

Fundamental analysis is commonly used by long-term investors who seek to identify assets with solid underlying value and growth potential. It helps investors make informed investment decisions based on the fundamental factors influencing the asset's value rather than relying solely on short-term market trends or speculation.

Economic indicators and their impact on currency values.

Economic indicators play a crucial role in determining currency values as they provide insights into the overall health and performance of an economy. Currency values are influenced by a variety of economic indicators, and changes in these indicators can impact the supply and demand dynamics of a currency. Here are some key economic indicators and their impact on currency values:

Gross Domestic Product (GDP): GDP measures the total value of goods and services produced within a country's borders. A strong GDP growth rate is generally associated with a robust economy and can lead to increased investment and demand for the country's currency.

Interest Rates: Central banks adjust interest rates to control inflation and stimulate or cool down economic activity. Higher interest rates tend to attract foreign investment as they offer better returns, leading to an increased demand for the currency. Conversely, lower interest rates may reduce foreign investment and weaken the currency.

Inflation Rate: Inflation measures the rate at which the general price level of goods and services in an economy is increasing. High inflation erodes the purchasing power of a currency, reducing its value. Central banks often raise interest rates to combat inflation, which can strengthen the currency.

Employment Data: Employment indicators, such as the unemployment rate and non-farm payrolls, provide insights into the labor market conditions. Lower unemployment rates and strong job growth can indicate a healthy economy and increase confidence in the currency.

Trade Balance: The trade balance reflects the difference between a country's exports and imports. A positive trade balance (surplus) indicates that a country is exporting more than it imports, which can strengthen the currency. Conversely, a negative trade balance (deficit) may weaken the currency.

Consumer Confidence: Consumer confidence measures the sentiment and optimism of consumers regarding the state of the economy. Higher consumer confidence levels often lead to increased consumer spending, which can stimulate economic growth and support the currency.

Political and Geopolitical Factors: Political stability, government policies, and geopolitical events can have significant impacts on currency values. Political uncertainty or instability can weaken a currency as investors may seek safer alternatives.

It's important to note that the impact of economic indicators on currency values is not always straightforward and can be influenced by other factors such as market expectations, monetary policy decisions, and global market conditions. Traders and investors closely monitor economic indicators and their potential impact on currency values to make informed trading decisions.

News events and their influence on the Forex market.

News events can have a significant influence on the Forex market as they can create volatility, shape market sentiment, and drive currency movements. Traders closely monitor news events to identify potential trading opportunities and manage risk. Here are some key points regarding the influence of news events on the Forex market:

Economic Data Releases: Economic indicators, such as GDP, employment data, inflation reports, and central bank announcements, can have a substantial impact on currency values. Better-than-expected or stronger economic data can strengthen a currency, while weaker-than-expected data can weaken it. Traders analyze these releases and compare them to market expectations to gauge the market's reaction.

Central Bank Decisions: Monetary policy decisions and statements from central banks, including interest rate changes, policy outlook, and guidance, can significantly impact currency values. Central bank actions influence interest rate differentials, which affect capital flows and currency demand.

Traders closely follow central bank meetings and statements for clues about future policy direction.

Geopolitical Events: Political developments, such as elections, government policy changes, geopolitical tensions, and trade disputes, can create volatility in the Forex market. Uncertainty and instability resulting from geopolitical events can lead to increased risk aversion, impacting currency values. Traders assess the potential implications of such events on the global economy and currencies involved.

It is essential for traders to have a reliable news source and stay informed about scheduled economic releases and significant events that could impact the Forex market. They often incorporate news analysis into their trading strategies and use risk management techniques to navigate potential market volatility associated with news events.

Geopolitical factors and their relevance to currency movements.

Geopolitical factors play a crucial role in shaping currency movements as they reflect the impact of political events and developments on the global economy. Changes in geopolitical dynamics can create uncertainty, affect investor sentiment, and influence the demand and supply of currencies. Here are some key points regarding the relevance of geopolitical factors to currency movements:

Political Stability: The stability of a country's political environment is an important factor in currency movements. Currencies of politically stable countries often attract investment and maintain their value. Conversely, political unrest, conflicts, or regime changes can lead to volatility and weaken a currency as investors seek safer alternatives.

Trade Relations and Policies: Geopolitical events, such as trade disputes, tariffs, and changes in trade policies, can significantly impact currency values. Negotiations or conflicts related to international trade agreements can create uncertainty and affect the economies of countries involved. Currency movements may reflect the perceived winners or losers of these events.

Monetary Policy: Geopolitical factors can influence the monetary policies of countries. Central banks may adjust interest rates, implement stimulus measures, or alter their currency interventions in response to geopolitical developments. Changes in monetary policy can impact currency values, as interest rate differentials affect capital flows and investor demand for currencies.

Note that the relationship between geopolitical factors and currency movements can be complex and multifaceted. Currency markets are influenced by a wide range of factors, including economic fundamentals, market sentiment, and technical analysis. Traders and investors carefully monitor geopolitical events and their potential implications on currencies to make informed trading decisions and manage risk effectively.

Using economic calendars and news sources for analysis.

Using economic calendars and news sources is essential for conducting analysis in financial markets, including the Forex market. These tools provide valuable information on scheduled economic releases, news events, and developments that can impact market sentiment and influence currency movements. Here's how you can effectively utilize economic calendars and news sources for analysis:

Economic Calendars:
Stay updated: Economic calendars provide a schedule of upcoming economic releases, including indicators like GDP, employment data, inflation reports, central bank meetings, and speeches. Stay updated with the latest calendar to know when important data releases are expected.
Identify high-impact events: Focus on high-impact economic events that are likely to have a significant impact on currency values. These events often

include interest rate decisions, employment reports, and central bank announcements.

Analyze market expectations: Economic calendars often include market consensus or forecasts for each data release. Compare the actual data with market expectations to understand if the outcome is better or worse than anticipated, which can drive market reactions.

Monitor historical data: Track historical data releases to identify patterns or trends that can help you anticipate potential market reactions. Understand how specific economic indicators have influenced currency movements in the past.

Plan your trading strategy: Incorporate economic calendar events into your trading strategy. Determine which events are relevant to your trading approach, set entry and exit levels, and consider implementing risk management techniques to manage potential volatility.

News Sources:

- Reliable news sources: Rely on reputable news sources that provide accurate and timely information. This can include financial news websites, news agencies, specialized Forex news providers, and official statements from central banks or government institutions.

- Market analysis and commentary: Pay attention to market analysis and commentary from financial experts and analysts. These insights can help you understand the potential impact of news events on the market and gain different perspectives.

- Breaking news: Stay updated with breaking news that can impact the financial markets. Important geopolitical events, policy announcements, or unexpected economic developments can create volatility and present trading opportunities.

- Global news coverage: Keep an eye on news sources that cover global events as geopolitical factors can significantly influence currency movements. Stay informed about political developments, trade disputes, and other relevant events that may impact market sentiment.

- Consider multiple sources: Cross-reference information from different news sources to ensure accuracy and reduce the risk of relying on biased or misleading information. Different sources may provide varying viewpoints and insights.

By utilizing economic calendars and news sources, traders and investors can stay informed about important economic releases, events, and developments that can impact currency values. This information can help shape trading strategies, manage risk, and make well-informed trading decisions in the dynamic Forex market.

Technical Analysis:

Introduction to charts and timeframes.

- Charts and timeframes are important tools used in technical analysis to analyze and interpret historical price data in financial markets, including the Forex market. They provide visual representations of price movements over time and help traders identify patterns, trends, support and resistance levels, and potential trading opportunities. Here's an introduction to charts and timeframes:

Charts:

Price data visualization: Charts represent the historical price data of an asset using graphical elements, such as lines, bars, or candlesticks. The vertical axis of the chart represents the price scale, while the horizontal axis represents the time scale.

Different types of charts: The most common types of charts used in technical analysis include line charts, bar charts, and candlestick charts. Each type has its own advantages and provides different levels of detail and information.

- Line charts: Line charts connect closing prices over time, forming a line that shows the general direction of the price movement. They provide a simplified view of the price trend and are useful for identifying long-term trends.

Here's an example of a line chart;

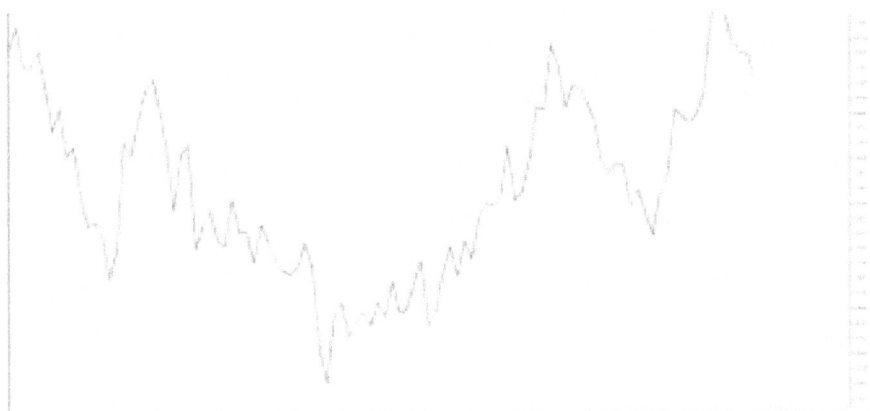

- Bar charts: Bar charts display a vertical line (bar) for each time period, with the top indicating the highest price, the bottom indicating the lowest price, and a horizontal line on each side representing the opening and closing prices.

Below is an example of Bar chart;

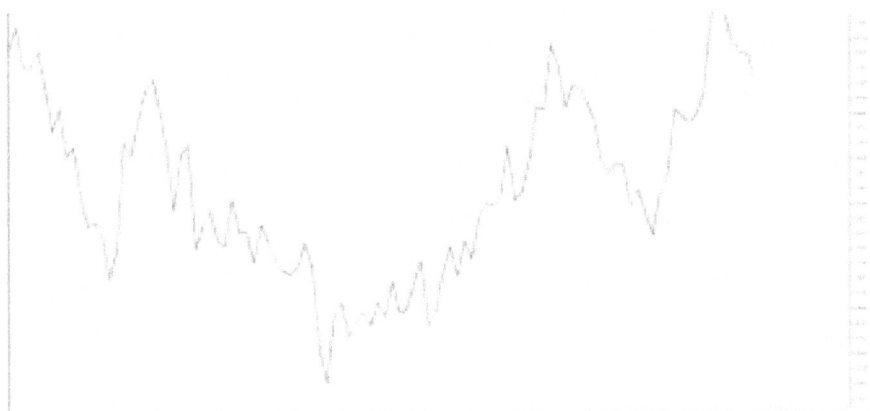

- Candlestick charts: Candlestick charts provide more detailed information compared to line and bar charts. Each candlestick represents a specific time period and displays the opening, closing, high, and low prices. The body of the candlestick is filled or hollow, indicating whether the closing price was higher or lower than the opening price.

Here's an example of candlestick chart;

Timeframes:
- Timeframe selection: Timeframes refer to the duration or interval of each candlestick or bar on the chart. Commonly used timeframes include minutes (e.g., 1-minute, 5-minute), hours (e.g., 1-hour, 4-hour), daily, weekly, and monthly.
- Short-term timeframes: Shorter timeframes, such as 1-minute or 5-minute charts, provide more detailed information about intraday price movements. They are often used by day traders or scalpers to identify short-term trading opportunities.
- Long-term timeframes: Longer timeframes, such as daily, weekly, or monthly charts, provide a broader view of price trends and are useful for identifying long-term market trends and making more strategic trading decisions.
- Multiple timeframes analysis: Traders often use multiple timeframes simultaneously to gain a comprehensive view of the market. For example, they may use a longer-term timeframe to identify the overall trend and a shorter-term timeframe to fine-tune entry and exit points.
- Timeframe selection considerations: The choice of timeframe depends on the trader's trading style, goals, and time availability. Shorter timeframes require more active monitoring and may be suitable for

day traders, while longer timeframes are more suitable for swing traders or position traders.

Charts and timeframes are valuable tools for technical analysis, allowing traders to visually interpret price data and identify trading opportunities. Traders should choose the appropriate chart type and timeframe that align with their trading strategies and goals. Regular analysis of charts across different timeframes can provide a comprehensive understanding of price movements and enhance trading decisions.

Key chart patterns: support and resistance, trendlines, channels.

- Key chart patterns are important tools used in technical analysis to identify potential price reversals, trend directions, and trading opportunities. Here are three key chart patterns: support and resistance, trendlines, and channels:

Support and Resistance:
- Support: Support is a price level at which buying pressure is expected to be strong enough to prevent further price declines. It acts as a floor for the price, where demand exceeds supply, and can potentially lead to a price bounce or reversal.

Below is an example of support level;

- Resistance: Resistance is a price level at which selling pressure is expected to be strong enough to prevent further price increases. It acts as a ceiling for the price, where supply exceeds demand, and can potentially lead to a price pullback or reversal.

Below is an example of Resistance level;

- Identification: Support and resistance levels can be identified by looking for areas where the price has historically reversed or encountered difficulty breaking through. These levels can be horizontal, forming a price range, or diagonal, indicating a trendline acting as support or resistance.

Below is an example;

- **Trading implications:** Traders often look for opportunities to buy near support levels and sell near resistance levels. Breakouts above resistance or below support can indicate potential trend continuation or reversal, respectively.

Below is an example;

Trendlines:
- **Upward trendline: An upward trendline is drawn by connecting higher swing lows in an uptrend. It acts as a visual representation of the trend's support line. As long as the price remains above the upward trendline, the uptrend is considered intact.**

Below is an example;

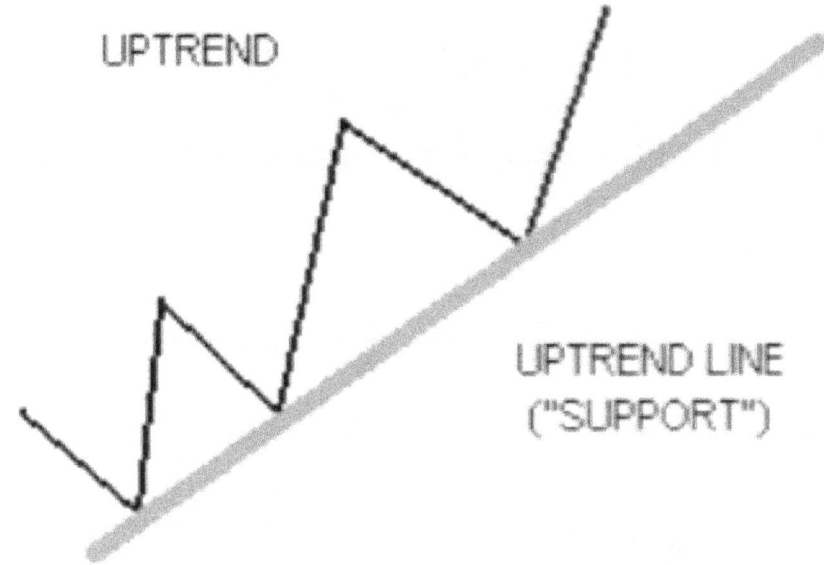

UPTREND

UPTREND LINE
("SUPPORT")

- Downward trendline: A downward trendline is drawn by connecting lower swing highs in a downtrend. It acts as a visual representation of the trend's resistance line. As long as the price remains below the downward trendline, the downtrend is considered intact.

Below is an example;

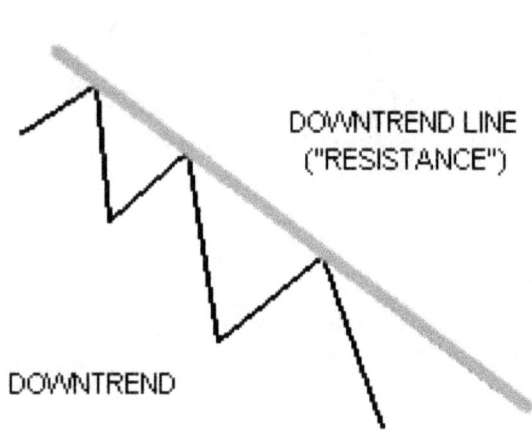

DOWNTREND LINE ("RESISTANCE")

DOWNTREND

- Identification: Trendlines are drawn by connecting consecutive swing highs or swing lows, depending on the trend direction. At least two points are required to draw a trendline, but the more touches, the stronger the trendline is considered.

- Trading implications: Trendlines can help traders identify potential entry and exit points. Buying near an upward trendline or selling near a downward trendline can present opportunities to trade in the direction of the trend. Breakouts or violations of trendlines can indicate potential trend reversals.

Channels:
- Ascending channel: An ascending channel consists of an upward

trendline acting as support and an upward parallel line acting as resistance. The price moves within the channel, making higher swing highs and higher swing lows.

Below is an example;

- Descending channel: A descending channel consists of a downward trendline acting as resistance and a downward parallel line acting as support. The price moves within the channel, making lower swing highs and lower swing lows.

Below is an example;

- Identification: Channels are drawn by connecting trendlines that contain price action within parallel lines. The more touches each trendline has, the stronger the channel is considered.

- Trading implications: Traders can look for potential trading opportunities within channels. Buying near the lower trendline (support) and selling near the upper trendline (resistance) can provide potential entry and exit points. Breakouts above the upper trendline or below the lower trendline can indicate potential trend continuation or reversal, respectively.

These key chart patterns are widely used by technical analysts to identify potential trading opportunities, determine stop-loss levels, and assess the strength of trends. It is important to combine chart patterns with other technical indicators and tools to confirm signals and increase the probability of successful trades.

Popular technical indicators: moving averages, oscillators, etc.

Popular technical indicators are widely used by traders and analysts to analyze price data, identify trends, generate trading signals, and make informed trading decisions. Here are a few examples of popular technical indicators:

Moving Averages (MA):
- Simple Moving Average (SMA): SMA calculates the average price over a specified period, smoothing out price fluctuations. It helps identify the direction and strength of a trend.

- Exponential Moving Average (EMA): EMA assigns more weight to recent prices, making it more responsive to recent price changes. It is commonly used to identify short-term trends and generate trading signals.

Oscillators:

- Relative Strength Index (RSI): RSI measures the speed and change of price movements. It oscillates between 0 and 100, with readings above 70 indicating overbought conditions and readings below 30 indicating oversold conditions.

- Moving Average Convergence Divergence (MACD): MACD consists of two lines, the MACD line and the signal line, along with a histogram. It helps identify potential trend reversals, bullish or bearish crossovers, and divergence between price and indicator.

- Stochastic Oscillator: The Stochastic oscillator compares the closing price of an asset to its price range over a specified period. It provides information about overbought and oversold conditions, as well as potential trend reversals.

Bollinger Bands: Bollinger Bands consist of a simple moving average and two standard deviation bands above and below it. They help identify volatility, overbought and oversold conditions, and potential price breakouts.

Fibonacci Retracement: Fibonacci retracement levels are horizontal lines drawn on a chart to identify potential support and resistance levels based on the Fibonacci sequence. Traders use them to determine possible areas of price reversals or continuation.

Ichimoku Cloud: The Ichimoku Cloud is a comprehensive indicator that provides information about support and resistance levels, trend direction, and potential trading signals. It consists of multiple components, including the Cloud (Kumo), Tenkan-Sen, Kijun-Sen, and Chikou Span.

Volume Indicators: Volume indicators, such as On-Balance Volume (OBV) and Volume Weighted Average Price (VWAP), provide insights into the trading volume accompanying price movements. They can help confirm the strength of trends and identify potential reversals.

These are just a few examples of popular technical indicators used by traders. Each indicator has its own strengths, limitations, and interpretation techniques. It is important to understand how to use them effectively and to combine them with other indicators or tools to enhance analysis and generate more robust trading signals.

Candlestick patterns and their interpretation.

Candlestick patterns are visual representations of price movements on a chart using candlestick shapes and formations. Traders use candlestick patterns to identify potential trend reversals, continuation patterns, and trading signals. Here are some commonly observed candlestick patterns and their interpretations:

Bullish Candlestick Patterns:
- Hammer: A hammer candlestick has a small body and a long lower shadow, with little to no upper shadow. It forms after a downtrend and suggests a potential bullish reversal. It indicates that buyers are stepping in and pushing the price higher.

- Bullish Engulfing: A bullish engulfing pattern occurs when a larger bullish candle fully engulfs the previous smaller bearish candle. It signifies a shift from selling pressure to buying pressure and suggests a bullish reversal.

Below is an example;

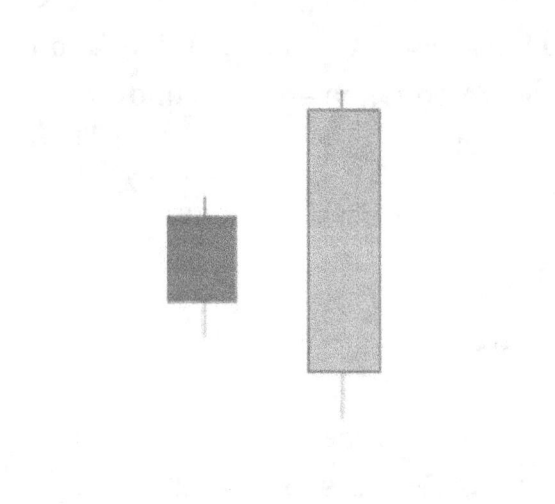

- Morning Star: The morning star pattern consists of three candles: a large bearish candle, a small candle with a lower range, and a large bullish candle. It forms after a downtrend and indicates a potential trend reversal to the upside.

Below is an example;

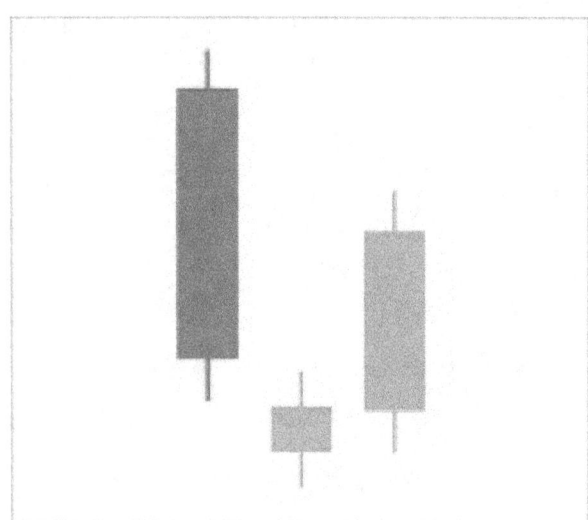

- Piercing Line: The piercing line pattern occurs when a bullish candle closes more than halfway above the previous bearish candle. It suggests a potential bullish reversal, indicating that buyers are gaining strength.

Below is an example;

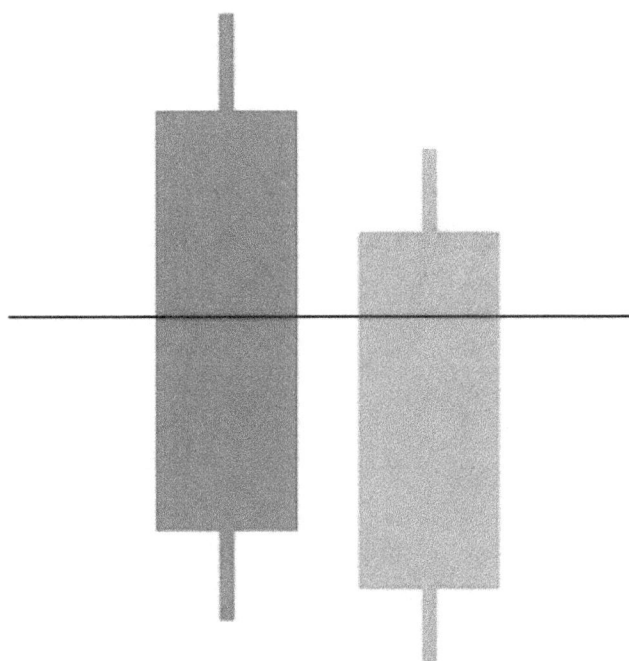

Bearish Candlestick Patterns:
- Shooting Star: A shooting star candlestick has a small body and a long upper shadow, with little to no lower shadow. It forms after an uptrend and indicates a potential bearish reversal. It suggests that sellers are entering the market and pushing the price lower.

Below is an example;

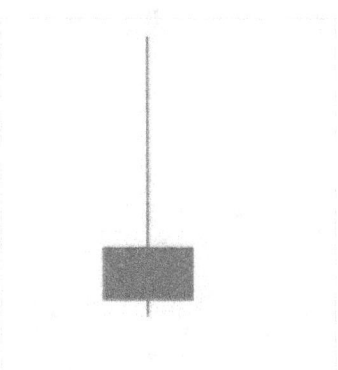

- Bearish Engulfing: A bearish engulfing pattern occurs when a larger bearish candle fully engulfs the previous smaller bullish candle. It signifies a shift from buying pressure to selling pressure and suggests a bearish reversal.

Below is an example;

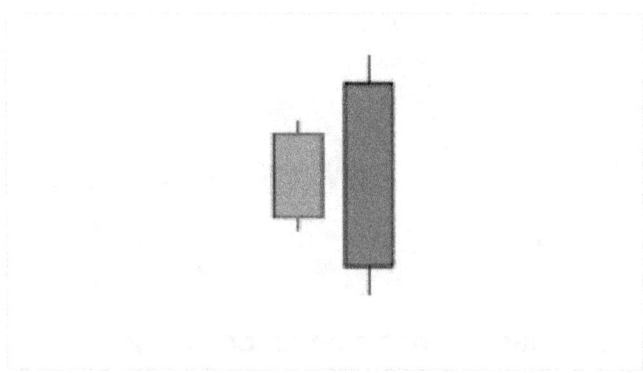

- Evening Star: The evening star pattern consists of three candles: a large bullish candle, a small candle with a higher range, and a large bearish candle. It forms after an uptrend and indicates a potential trend reversal to the downside.

Below is an example;

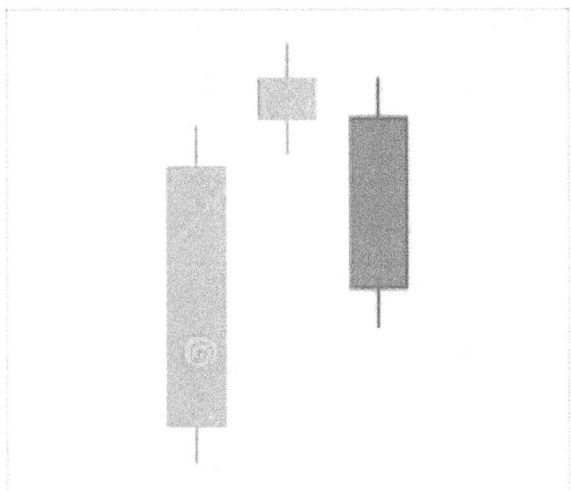

- Dark Cloud Cover: The dark cloud cover pattern occurs when a bearish candle closes more than halfway below the previous bullish candle. It suggests a potential bearish reversal, indicating that sellers are gaining strength.

Below is an example;

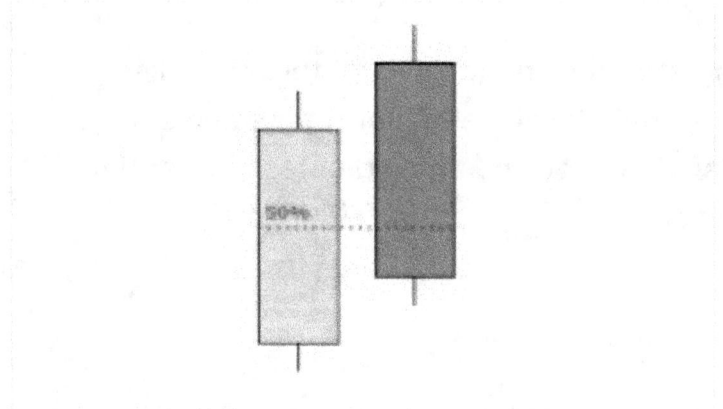

Developing a Trading Strategy:

Setting trading goals and defining risk tolerance.

- Setting trading goals and defining risk tolerance are crucial steps in developing a trading plan and managing your trading activities effectively. Here's an overview of how to set trading goals and define risk tolerance:

Setting Trading Goals:
- Define your objectives: Start by identifying what you aim to achieve through trading. Your goals could include generating consistent profits, growing your trading account, preserving capital, or learning and improving your trading skills.
- Make them specific and measurable: Set clear and quantifiable goals. For example, specify a target return on investment (ROI) percentage, a monthly profit target, or a desired number of successful trades.
- Consider timeframes: Determine whether your goals are short-term (e.g., daily or weekly targets), medium-term (e.g., monthly or quarterly targets), or long-term (e.g., annual or multi-year targets).
- Realistic and achievable: Set goals that are realistic and align with your trading skills, experience, and available resources. Unrealistic goals can lead to frustration and poor decision-making.
- Write them down: Document your goals and keep them visible. This helps you stay focused and committed to achieving them.

Defining Risk Tolerance:
- Assess your risk appetite: Evaluate how much risk you are willing and comfortable to take. Risk tolerance varies from trader to trader based on factors such as financial situation, trading experience, psychological resilience, and personal preferences.
- Determine risk per trade: Decide on the maximum amount or percentage of capital you are willing to risk on each trade. This helps you manage the downside and protect your trading account from

significant losses.

- Consider position sizing: Based on your risk per trade, determine the appropriate position size for each trade. Position sizing helps you control risk by adjusting the number of lots or shares traded.
- Set stop-loss levels: Implement stop-loss orders to automatically exit a trade if the price moves against you beyond a predefined level. Stop-loss orders help limit potential losses and protect your capital.
- Regularly review and reassess: Your risk tolerance may change over time due to various factors. It's important to periodically reassess your risk tolerance and make necessary adjustments to your trading plan.

Risk Management:
- Implement a risk management strategy: Develop a risk management plan that includes guidelines for determining trade size, setting stop-loss levels, and managing overall portfolio risk. This helps ensure that your risk exposure is controlled and within your predefined risk tolerance.
- Diversify your trades: Avoid putting all your capital into a single trade or market. Diversification across different instruments, sectors, or currencies can help spread risk and reduce the impact of individual trade outcomes.
- Regularly review and analyze: Continuously monitor and review your trading activities, assess the effectiveness of your risk management measures, and make adjustments if needed. Learn from both winning and losing trades to improve your risk management skills.

Setting trading goals and defining risk tolerance are personal and individual processes. It's important to be honest with yourself, understand your financial situation, and continuously evaluate and adjust your goals and risk tolerance as needed. Remember that trading involves inherent risks, and a well-defined trading plan with appropriate risk management measures can help you navigate the markets more effectively and increase your chances of long-term success.

Choosing a trading style (scalping, day trading, swing trading, etc.).

Choosing a trading style is an important decision that depends on your trading preferences, available time, risk tolerance, and market conditions. Here's an overview of different trading styles to consider:

Scalping:
- Scalping involves making frequent trades to capture small price movements within short timeframes, typically holding positions for seconds to minutes.
- Traders who scalp aim to profit from small price fluctuations and rely on high trading volume and quick execution.
- Scalping requires intense focus, active monitoring of price charts, and a robust trading platform with low latency.
- It may suit traders who prefer a fast-paced, high-frequency trading approach and can dedicate significant time to actively trading throughout the day.

Day Trading:
- Day trading involves opening and closing trades within the same trading day, with the goal of capturing intraday price movements.
- Day traders typically focus on short-term trends, use technical analysis, and make multiple trades during a single trading session.
- They may utilize various trading strategies and indicators to identify entry and exit points.
- Day trading requires monitoring price charts, market news, and intraday market dynamics.
- It may suit traders who can dedicate several hours during the trading day to actively monitor and manage their trades.

Swing Trading:
- Swing trading involves holding trades for a few days to several weeks to capture medium-term price swings within a trend.
- Swing traders aim to identify and take advantage of price reversals, using technical analysis and chart patterns to time their entries and exits.

- They focus on capturing larger price moves compared to scalpers or day traders.
- Swing trading allows for more flexibility in terms of time commitment compared to scalping or day trading.
- It may suit traders who prefer a more relaxed trading approach, can dedicate time for analysis and monitoring, and are comfortable with holding positions overnight.

Position Trading:
- Position trading involves taking longer-term trades that can last weeks, months, or even years.
- Position traders focus on capturing major trends and market movements, often relying on fundamental analysis and macroeconomic factors.
- They aim to profit from significant price movements and are willing to tolerate larger drawdowns and longer holding periods.
- Position trading requires a broader market perspective, patience, and the ability to ride out short-term volatility.
- It may suit traders with a longer-term outlook, who can dedicate less time for active trading and prefer to focus on fundamental analysis.

It's important to note that these trading styles are not mutually exclusive, and some traders may combine elements of different styles based on their preferences and market conditions. It's recommended to experiment and practice with different styles on a demo account or with small trading sizes before committing significant capital. Additionally, adapting your trading style over time based on market conditions and personal circumstances is a normal part of the trading journey.

Building a trading plan: entry and exit rules, risk management.

Building a trading plan is an essential step for any forex trader. It helps you establish a clear framework for your trading activities, including entry and exit rules and risk management strategies. Here are some key components to consider when creating a trading plan:

Define your trading goals: Determine your financial goals, whether they are short-term or long-term, and be specific about what you aim to achieve through forex trading.

Choose a trading strategy: Select a trading strategy that aligns with your goals, risk tolerance, and trading style. Common strategies include trend following, range trading, breakout trading, and fundamental analysis.

Entry rules: Develop a set of criteria that will guide you on when to enter a trade. This may include technical indicators, chart patterns, or fundamental factors. Define specific conditions that need to be met before you initiate a trade.

Exit rules: Determine when you will exit a trade to take profits or cut losses. This can be based on predetermined price levels, technical indicators, trailing stops, or fundamental changes in the market. Having a clear exit strategy helps you avoid emotional decision-making.

Risk management: Establish risk management guidelines to protect your capital. Determine the maximum amount of capital you are willing to risk on each trade (e.g., a percentage of your trading account) and set stop-loss orders to limit potential losses. Consider using proper position sizing techniques to manage risk effectively.

Money management: Decide on the amount of capital you will allocate to each trade. Proper money management involves not risking too much on a single trade, diversifying your portfolio, and managing leverage effectively.

Trading psychology: Recognize the psychological aspect of trading and develop strategies to manage emotions such as fear, greed, and impatience. Maintaining discipline and sticking to your trading plan can help you avoid impulsive decisions.

Review and adapt: Regularly review your trading plan and make adjustments as needed. Monitor your trading performance, identify areas for improvement, and refine your strategies over time.

Remember, a trading plan is a dynamic document that should evolve as you gain experience and the market conditions change. It is important to adhere to your plan consistently and avoid making impulsive decisions based on emotions or short-term market fluctuations.

Backtesting and optimizing a trading strategy.

Backtesting and optimizing a trading strategy are crucial steps to evaluate the performance and potential profitability of your strategy before applying it to live trading. Here's a general outline of the process:

Define the strategy: Clearly define the rules and parameters of your trading strategy, including entry and exit criteria, indicators, timeframes, and risk management rules. Ensure that the strategy is well-defined and specific.

Historical data selection: Obtain historical price data for the currency pairs you intend to trade. The data should cover a sufficiently long period to capture different market conditions.

Manual backtesting: Manually apply your strategy to the historical data, following the defined rules and taking note of the trades you would have executed. This process helps you understand how your strategy would have performed in the past. Keep track of the entry and exit points, profit or loss for each trade, and overall performance metrics.

Automated backtesting: To enhance efficiency, you can use specialized software or trading platforms that offer backtesting capabilities. These tools allow you to input your strategy rules and run the backtest automatically on historical data. The software will generate performance reports and metrics, such as win rate, average profit/loss per trade, maximum drawdown, and risk-reward ratios.

Performance analysis: Evaluate the performance of your strategy by analyzing the backtest results. Consider key metrics such as profitability, drawdowns, and risk-adjusted returns. Assess the strategy's consistency, stability, and responsiveness to different market conditions.

Optimization: If the initial backtest results are not satisfactory, you may need to optimize your strategy. This involves adjusting the parameters or rules to find more favorable settings. However, be cautious not to over-optimize, as it can lead to curve-fitting and poor performance in live trading. Use optimization techniques sparingly and with a focus on robustness.

Walk-forward testing: After optimizing your strategy, conduct a walk-forward test to validate its performance on a separate out-of-sample dataset. This helps assess if the optimized strategy has a reasonable chance of success in real-time trading.

Iteration and refinement: Repeat the backtesting, optimization, and walk-forward testing process as necessary. Continuously refine and improve your strategy based on the insights gained from the testing results.

Remember that backtesting is not a guarantee of future performance, as market conditions can change. It is crucial to remain cautious and realistic about the limitations of backtesting. Regularly review and update your trading strategy based on real-time market observations and ongoing performance analysis.

Risk Management and Psychology:

Understanding risk and reward.

- Understanding risk and reward is essential in forex trading as it directly impacts your profitability and risk management. Let's explore these concepts:

Risk: Risk refers to the potential for financial loss in a trade or investment. In forex trading, risk can arise from various factors, including market volatility, economic events, and unforeseen circumstances. It is crucial to assess and manage risk effectively to protect your trading capital.

Risk tolerance: Determine your risk tolerance level based on your financial situation, trading experience, and personal preferences. Assess how much capital you are willing to risk on each trade and set guidelines accordingly.

- Stop-loss orders: Implementing stop-loss orders is a common risk management technique. A stop-loss order is a predetermined price level at which you will exit a trade to limit potential losses. By setting a stop-loss order, you define the maximum amount you are willing to lose on a trade.
- Position sizing: Proper position sizing helps control risk. Determine the appropriate position size for each trade based on your risk tolerance and the distance between your entry point and stop-loss level. Avoid risking too much of your capital on a single trade, as it can lead to significant losses.
- Risk-reward ratio: The risk-reward ratio compares the potential profit of a trade to the potential loss. It represents the relationship between the risk you take and the reward you expect. A favorable risk-reward ratio means that the potential reward is higher than the risk, indicating a potentially profitable trade.

Reward: Reward refers to the potential gain or profit from a trade. In forex trading, your reward is determined by various factors, such as the price movement of the currency pair, your entry and exit points, and the size of your position.

- Profit target: Set a profit target for each trade, which represents the desired level of profit you aim to achieve. It can be determined based on technical analysis, support and resistance levels, or other indicators.
- Take-profit orders: Implementing take-profit orders allows you to automatically exit a trade when the price reaches your desired profit target. Take-profit orders help lock in profits and avoid the temptation of staying in a trade for too long, potentially risking a reversal.
- Reward potential assessment: Before entering a trade, assess the potential reward relative to the risk you are taking. Ensure that the potential profit justifies the risk you are exposing your capital to. A favorable risk-reward ratio is typically sought after to increase the likelihood of profitable trades.
- Balancing risk and reward is crucial in forex trading. It involves managing potential losses through risk management techniques while seeking profitable opportunities with a favorable risk-reward ratio. Remember to regularly review and adjust your risk management strategies as market conditions and your trading performance evolve.

Setting stop-loss and take-profit levels.

Setting stop-loss and take-profit levels is an important aspect of risk management in forex trading. These orders help you control potential losses and lock in profits. Here's how you can determine and set appropriate stop-loss and take-profit levels:

Stop-loss levels:
- Support and resistance: Identify key support and resistance levels on the price chart. Set your stop-loss level below the support level for long trades and above the resistance level for short trades. This helps protect your position if the price moves against you.
- Volatility-based stops: Consider using volatility-based indicators such

as Average True Range (ATR) to determine stop-loss levels. ATR measures the average price range of a currency pair over a specified period. Setting your stop-loss beyond the average range accounts for market volatility and reduces the chances of being stopped out prematurely.

- Technical analysis: Utilize technical analysis tools such as trend lines, moving averages, or chart patterns to identify potential reversal points or invalidation levels. Set your stop-loss level beyond these levels to allow for price fluctuations while still protecting your position.
- Money management: Determine the maximum amount of capital you are willing to risk on a trade. Calculate the distance between your entry point and potential stop-loss level based on this risk tolerance. Adjust your position size accordingly to ensure you stay within your predetermined risk limits.

Take-profit levels:
- Price targets: Identify key price levels where you expect the market to reach based on your analysis, such as resistance levels, Fibonacci retracement levels, or previous highs/lows. Set your take-profit level near these targets to secure profits if the price moves in your favor.
- Reward potential assessment: Assess the potential reward relative to the risk you are taking. Aim for a favorable risk-reward ratio where the potential profit justifies the risk. Consider setting your take-profit level at a distance that allows for a desirable reward-to-risk ratio.
- Trailing stops: In a trending market, you can utilize trailing stops to lock in profits as the price moves in your favor. A trailing stop adjusts your stop-loss level dynamically, trailing the price at a fixed distance. It allows you to capture more significant gains while protecting against potential reversals.
- Partial profit-taking: Another strategy is to take partial profits by closing a portion of your position at a predetermined level while letting the rest of the position run with a trailing stop. This approach allows you to secure some profits while still participating in potential further gains.

Remember, stop-loss and take-profit levels should be set based on your trading strategy, risk tolerance, and market analysis. Regularly review and adjust these levels as the market conditions change or when price targets are reached. Additionally, be aware that setting stop-loss and take-profit levels does not guarantee that they will be executed exactly as planned, as slippage or market gaps can occur, especially during highly volatile periods.

Position sizing and leverage.

Position sizing and leverage are critical factors in forex trading that determine the size of your trades and the amount of capital you allocate. Here's an overview of position sizing and leverage:

Position Sizing:
- Risk tolerance: Determine the maximum percentage of your trading account that you are willing to risk on a single trade. This is often referred to as the risk per trade or risk percentage. A common guideline is to risk between 1% and 3% of your trading capital per trade, but it ultimately depends on your risk tolerance and trading strategy.
- Stop-loss placement: Consider the distance between your entry point and stop-loss level to calculate the potential loss in the trade. This, along with your risk tolerance, can help determine the appropriate position size.
- Risk calculation: Calculate the position size based on the risk per trade and the potential loss. For example, if you have a $10,000 trading account and are willing to risk 2% ($200) on a trade with a 50-pip stop-loss, and each pip represents $1, your position size would be $4 per pip ($200 divided by 50).
- Lot size: In forex trading, position sizes are typically measured in lots. A standard lot represents 100,000 units of the base currency. Mini lots (10,000 units) and micro lots (1,000 units) are also common. Adjust your position size accordingly based on your account size and risk management guidelines.

Leverage:

- Leverage definition: Leverage allows traders to control larger positions in the market with a smaller amount of capital. It is expressed as a ratio, such as 1:50, 1:100, or higher, indicating how much you can multiply your trading capital.

- Margin requirement: Leverage is closely tied to margin requirements. Margin is the amount of money you need to have in your trading account to open and maintain a position. It is a fraction of the total value of the position. The margin requirement is typically a percentage determined by your broker, based on the leverage ratio and the currency pair being traded.

- Considerations for leverage: While leverage can amplify potential profits, it also magnifies losses. Higher leverage increases the risk of significant drawdowns and the potential for margin calls if trades move against you. It is important to use leverage judiciously and consider its implications on risk management.

- Risk management with leverage: Adjust your position size based on the leverage used and the margin requirement. Higher leverage requires smaller position sizes to keep risk within your predetermined limits. Avoid excessive leverage that can put your trading account at risk.

- Leverage regulations: Be aware that leverage regulations vary by country and jurisdiction. Different financial authorities may impose restrictions on leverage ratios available to retail traders to protect them from excessive risk. Familiarize yourself with the applicable regulations in your region.

It is important to note that position sizing and leverage decisions should be made with caution. Always prioritize risk management and ensure that you have a thorough understanding of the potential risks involved. Regularly assess and adjust your position sizing and leverage based on your trading performance, risk tolerance, and evolving market conditions.

Emotion control and maintaining discipline.

Emotion control and maintaining discipline are vital for successful forex trading. Emotions can often lead to impulsive decisions and deviations from your trading plan. Here are some strategies to help you manage emotions and maintain discipline:

Establish a trading plan: Develop a well-defined trading plan that includes your entry and exit rules, risk management strategies, and overall trading goals. Having a plan in place helps you stay focused and reduces the likelihood of emotional decision-making.

Stick to your trading plan: Once you have a trading plan, follow it consistently. Avoid making impulsive trades or deviating from your established rules based on short-term market fluctuations or emotional reactions. Trust in the process and the analysis that went into creating your plan.

Practice self-awareness: Be aware of your emotions while trading. Recognize common emotional responses such as fear, greed, and impatience. Understanding your emotions allows you to identify when they are influencing your decision-making and take steps to manage them effectively.

Use proper risk management techniques: Implement risk management strategies, such as setting stop-loss orders and adhering to proper position sizing, to limit potential losses. Knowing that you have measures in place to protect your capital can help reduce emotional stress and impulsive behavior.

Take regular breaks: Forex trading can be mentally demanding. Take breaks during trading sessions to relax, clear your mind, and regain focus. Stepping away from the charts for a while can help prevent emotional exhaustion and decision-making biases.

Avoid overtrading: Overtrading, driven by impatience or the desire to recoup losses quickly, can lead to poor decision-making. Stick to your trading plan and avoid entering trades that don't meet your criteria. Quality over quantity is essential in forex trading.

Practice risk tolerance and acceptance: Understand that losses are a natural part of trading. Embrace the fact that not all trades will be winners, and losses are opportunities to learn and improve. Develop a mindset that accepts losses as a cost of doing business and focuses on long-term profitability.

Seek support and accountability: Consider joining a trading community or working with a mentor who can provide guidance, support, and accountability. Discussing your trades and emotions with like-minded individuals can help you gain perspective and stay disciplined.

Maintain a trading journal: Keep a detailed trading journal to track your trades, emotions, and thought processes. Reviewing past trades can help identify patterns, strengths, and weaknesses, allowing you to refine your trading approach and minimize emotional biases.

Managing emotions and maintaining discipline in forex trading is an ongoing process. It takes practice, self-awareness, and a commitment to sticking to your trading plan. By focusing on consistent execution and minimizing emotional influences, you increase your chances of long-term success in the forex market.

Practice and Demo Trading:

Opening a demo trading account.

Opening a demo trading account is an excellent way to practice and familiarize yourself with forex trading without risking real money. Here's a step-by-step guide to opening a demo trading account:

Choose a reliable forex broker: Research and select a reputable forex broker that offers demo accounts. Look for brokers that provide competitive trading conditions, a user-friendly platform, and a wide range of currency pairs.

Visit the broker's website: Go to the broker's official website and look for a section related to account types or registration.

Sign up for a demo account: Locate the option to open a demo account and click on it. You may be prompted to provide some personal information, such as your name, email address, and phone number. Some brokers may also require additional details for verification purposes.

Select account specifications: Choose the trading platform you want to use for your demo account. Popular platforms include MetaTrader 4 (MT4) and MetaTrader 5 (MT5). Specify the account currency (USD, EUR, etc.) and the initial demo balance you prefer.

Read and accept the terms and conditions: Carefully review the broker's terms and conditions, as well as any risk disclaimers associated with the demo account. Ensure that you understand the features and limitations of the demo account.

Download and install the trading platform: If the broker's platform is not web-based, you will usually be directed to download and install the trading platform onto your computer or mobile device. Follow the instructions provided by the broker to complete the installation.

Login to your demo account: Launch the trading platform and log in using the login credentials provided by the broker. Typically, you will use the username and password associated with your demo account. Some brokers may also provide you with a server address for logging in.

Explore the platform and practice trading: Familiarize yourself with the various features of the trading platform, including charting tools, order types, and risk management options. Use the demo account to practice executing trades, analyzing market conditions, and testing different strategies.

Monitor your progress and learn from your trades: Keep track of your trades, performance, and trading decisions. Analyze your results to identify strengths and areas for improvement. Use the demo account as a learning tool to refine your trading skills and strategies.

Demo trading account simulates real-market conditions, but the execution and pricing may differ slightly from a live trading account. Treat your demo account seriously, as it provides a valuable opportunity to gain experience and build confidence before transitioning to live trading with real money.

Using trading platforms and order types.

Using trading platforms and order types effectively is crucial in forex trading. Here's an overview of trading platforms and common order types:

Trading Platforms:
- MetaTrader 4 (MT4): MT4 is one of the most popular trading platforms for forex trading. It offers a wide range of tools, indicators, and charting capabilities. MT4 is known for its user-friendly interface and customizable features, making it suitable for both beginner and experienced traders.
- MetaTrader 5 (MT5): MT5 is the successor to MT4 and provides

enhanced features and capabilities. It offers additional asset classes beyond forex, including stocks, futures, and options. MT5 is designed to accommodate more advanced trading strategies and offers improved backtesting and analytical tools.

- Other platforms: Several brokers offer their proprietary trading platforms, which may have unique features and functionality. Examples include cTrader, NinjaTrader, and TradingView. When selecting a platform, consider factors such as ease of use, available tools, compatibility with your trading strategy, and the broker's reputation.

Order Types:
- Market Order: A market order is an instruction to buy or sell a currency pair at the prevailing market price. It is executed immediately at the best available price. Market orders are used when you want to enter or exit a trade quickly, without specifying a specific price.
- Limit Order: A limit order is an order to buy or sell a currency pair at a specific price or better. It allows you to set a desired entry or exit price. If the market reaches the specified price, the order is triggered and executed. Limit orders are useful when you want to enter a trade at a specific price or take profits at a predetermined level.
- Stop Order: A stop order becomes a market order once a specific price level is reached. A buy stop order is placed above the current market price, while a sell stop order is placed below it. Stop orders are commonly used to enter trades when the price breaks through a certain level or to limit losses by triggering a trade when the price moves against you.
- Stop-Loss Order: A stop-loss order is used to limit potential losses. It is an order placed to sell a currency pair at a specified price to minimize further losses if the trade goes against you. Stop-loss orders are typically placed below the entry price for long trades and above the entry price for short trades.
- Take-Profit Order: A take-profit order is used to lock in profits by automatically closing a trade at a predetermined price. It is placed above the entry price for long trades and below the entry price for short trades. Take-profit orders help you secure gains and avoid the

temptation of staying in a trade for too long.

These are just a few of the common order types available on most trading platforms. Depending on the platform and broker, you may also have access to advanced order types, such as trailing stops, OCO (One Cancels the Other), and IF-THEN orders. Familiarize yourself with the order types available on your chosen platform and use them strategically to execute your trading decisions effectively.

Practicing trade execution and analysis.

Practicing trade execution and analysis is essential for improving your forex trading skills. Here are some tips to help you practice and refine your trade execution and analysis:

Demo Trading: Utilize a demo trading account to practice executing trades in a risk-free environment. Experiment with different strategies, entry and exit points, and order types. Take note of the outcomes and analyze the effectiveness of your decisions.

Trade Journaling: Maintain a trade journal to record your trades, including the rationale behind each trade, entry and exit points, and any observations or lessons learned. Regularly review your trade journal to identify patterns, strengths, and weaknesses in your trading approach.

Backtesting: Backtesting involves applying your trading strategy to historical price data to see how it would have performed in the past. Use trading software or platforms with backtesting capabilities to simulate trades and analyze the results. This helps you assess the viability and profitability of your strategy before using it in real-time.

Consistent practice and analysis are key to improving your trade execution and analysis skills. Focus on identifying areas for improvement, maintaining discipline, and adapting your strategies based on market conditions. By dedicating time and effort to practice, you can enhance your trading abilities and increase your chances of success in the forex market.

Evaluating trading performance and making adjustments.

Evaluating your trading performance and making adjustments is a crucial aspect of becoming a successful forex trader. Here are some steps to help you evaluate your performance and make necessary adjustments:

Set Performance Metrics: Establish measurable performance metrics that align with your trading goals. Common metrics include win rate (percentage of winning trades), average gain per winning trade, average loss per losing trade, risk-to-reward ratio, and overall profitability. These metrics provide a quantitative basis for evaluating your performance.

Review Trade History: Regularly review your trade history and analyze the outcomes of your trades. Look for patterns and trends in your performance. Identify strengths and weaknesses in your trading strategy, risk management, and decision-making process. Assess if there are any recurring mistakes or areas for improvement.

Analyze Risk Management: Evaluate how effectively you manage risk in your trades. Assess if your position sizing, stop-loss levels, and risk per trade align with your risk tolerance and trading plan. If you notice that you are consistently experiencing large losses or high drawdowns, consider adjusting your risk management approach to protect your trading capital.

Assess Trade Execution: Evaluate your trade execution process. Assess if you are effectively entering and exiting trades according to your predetermined rules. Review factors such as slippage (the difference between the expected and executed price), trade timing, and order placement accuracy. If you notice consistent issues, consider refining your trade execution skills or adjusting your strategy.

Track Emotional Factors: Monitor your emotional state and how it influences your trading decisions. Assess if emotions such as fear, greed, or impatience affect your performance. Consider implementing techniques to manage emotions, such as mindfulness exercises, taking breaks, or using automated trading systems to remove emotional biases.

Keep a Trading Journal: Maintain a detailed trading journal to record your thoughts, observations, and lessons learned from each trade. Use the journal to review your decision-making process, analyze trade setups, and assess the effectiveness of your strategies. Regularly revisit your journal to identify patterns and areas for improvement.

Seek External Feedback: Consider seeking feedback from a trading mentor, experienced trader, or joining a trading community. Engage in discussions about your trades, seek advice, and learn from others' experiences. External perspectives can provide valuable insights and help you identify blind spots or areas where adjustments may be needed.

Make Incremental Adjustments: Based on your evaluation, make gradual adjustments to your trading approach. Avoid making drastic changes without sufficient evidence or thorough testing. Modify specific aspects of your strategy, risk management, or trade execution based on the insights gained from your evaluation. Monitor the impact of these adjustments and make further refinements as needed.

Continuously Educate Yourself: Stay updated with industry trends, new trading techniques, and market developments. Attend webinars, workshops, or seminars, read trading books, and follow reputable sources of financial news and analysis. Continuous education helps you stay adaptable and improve your trading skills.

Evaluating and adjusting your trading performance is an ongoing process. Regularly review your performance, seek improvement opportunities, and be open to learning from your experiences. By being proactive in evaluating and adjusting your trading approach, you can adapt to changing market conditions and enhance your long-term success as a forex trader.

Advanced Topics:

Advanced technical analysis techniques.

Advanced technical analysis is a branch of market analysis that involves using sophisticated tools, indicators, and chart patterns to forecast future price movements and make trading decisions. It builds upon the basic principles of technical analysis and delves deeper into complex techniques to gain insights into market trends and potential trading opportunities. Here are a few advanced technical analysis tools and concepts

Fibonacci retracement: Fibonacci retracement levels are horizontal lines that indicate potential support and resistance levels based on key Fibonacci ratios. Traders use these levels to identify areas where price corrections may end and the original trend could resume.

Elliott Wave Theory: This theory suggests that markets move in repetitive wave patterns, reflecting the psychology of market participants. It identifies trends, corrective waves, and wave extensions, helping traders anticipate potential turning points and trend continuations.

Oscillators: Oscillators, such as the Relative Strength Index (RSI) and Stochastic Oscillator, help identify overbought and oversold conditions in the market. These indicators provide insights into potential trend reversals and can be used to generate buy or sell signals.

Moving Averages: Moving averages smooth out price data to reveal trends more clearly. Advanced techniques involve using multiple moving averages of different periods to identify crossover signals, trend strength, and potential support/resistance levels.

Volume Analysis: Analyzing trading volume alongside price movements can provide valuable insights. Advanced volume analysis techniques, such as on-balance volume (OBV) or volume profile, help identify accumulation or distribution patterns and can validate the strength of price movements.

Candlestick Patterns: Candlestick patterns, such as doji, hammer, engulfing patterns, etc., provide visual representations of market sentiment. Advanced candlestick analysis involves recognizing complex patterns or combinations of candlesticks to anticipate potential trend reversals or continuations.

Chart Patterns: Advanced chart patterns, such as double tops/bottoms, head and shoulders, triangles, and wedges, can provide insights into future price movements. These patterns suggest potential trend reversals or continuations and are often used to identify entry and exit points.

It's important to note that while advanced technical analysis techniques can provide valuable insights, they are not foolproof and should be used in conjunction with other forms of analysis and risk management strategies. It's always advisable to combine technical analysis with fundamental analysis and consider the broader market context before making trading decisions.

Using automated trading systems (expert advisors).

Using automated trading systems, also known as expert advisors (EAs), is a popular approach in forex trading. EAs are software programs that are designed to automatically execute trades based on predefined trading rules and strategies. Traders can develop their own EAs or use pre-built ones available in the market.
Here are some key points to consider when using automated trading systems:

Strategy Development: Before using an EA, it's crucial to develop a robust trading strategy that aligns with your trading goals and risk tolerance. This involves defining entry and exit rules, money management parameters, and any other specific requirements. The trading strategy should be thoroughly tested and optimized before implementing it in an EA.

Backtesting: Backtesting involves running the EA on historical market data to assess its performance. This helps to gauge how the EA would have performed in different market conditions and provides insights into its strengths and weaknesses. It's important to conduct robust backtesting across various market scenarios to ensure the viability of the strategy.

Forward Testing: After successful backtesting, forward testing involves running the EA in a simulated or live trading environment with real-time data. This allows you to observe the EA's performance under real market conditions and assess its effectiveness and reliability. It's advisable to conduct forward testing for a reasonable duration before deploying the EA for live trading.

Risk Management: Proper risk management is essential when using automated trading systems. Determine the appropriate position sizing, stop-loss levels, and take-profit targets to control the risk exposure. It's crucial to monitor the performance of the EA regularly and make adjustments if needed to ensure risk is kept within acceptable levels.

Continuous Monitoring: Even though EAs operate automatically, it's essential to regularly monitor their performance and ensure they are functioning as intended. Market conditions can change, and adjustments may be required to adapt the EA to evolving market dynamics.

Selection of a Reliable Platform: Choose a reputable trading platform that supports the use of expert advisors. Different platforms have varying levels of functionality and compatibility with EAs. Ensure the platform is stable, secure, and provides the necessary tools and features for effective EA trading.

While automated trading systems can offer convenience and efficiency, it's important to note that they are not guaranteed to be profitable. Market conditions can change rapidly, and technical glitches or errors in the EA's programming can occur. Regular monitoring, periodic optimization, and continuous evaluation are crucial for successful EA trading.

Forex market correlations and intermarket analysis.

Forex market correlations and intermarket analysis are techniques used to examine relationships and interactions between different currency pairs and other financial markets. Understanding these correlations can provide insights into potential price movements and help traders make more informed trading decisions.

Here are key concepts related to forex market correlations and intermarket analysis:

Correlations: Forex market correlations refer to the statistical relationships between currency pairs. Positive correlation means that two currency pairs tend to move in the same direction, while negative correlation indicates they move in opposite directions. Correlations can be strong or weak, and they can be temporary or long-term.

Analyzing correlations can help traders in several ways:

Risk Management: Correlated currency pairs can expose traders to higher risk if positions are taken in multiple pairs moving in the same direction. Recognizing these correlations allows for better risk management and diversification.

Trading Strategies: Correlations can provide trading opportunities. For example, if two currency pairs have a strong positive correlation, a trader could use one pair as a leading indicator for the other, potentially gaining insights into entry or exit points.

Intermarket Analysis: Intermarket analysis involves studying the relationships between different financial markets, such as forex, stocks, commodities, and bonds. The idea is that markets are interconnected, and changes in one market can impact others.

Intermarket analysis can provide valuable insights:

Risk Sentiment: Certain assets, like safe-haven currencies or precious metals, tend to perform well during periods of market uncertainty or risk aversion. By analyzing other markets, traders can gauge overall risk sentiment, which can influence forex market movements.

Commodity Currencies: Some currencies, such as the Australian dollar (AUD) or Canadian dollar (CAD), are strongly influenced by commodity prices. Monitoring commodity markets can help identify potential trends or reversals in these currencies.

Interest Rates: Interest rate differentials between countries can significantly impact currency pairs. Monitoring bond markets and central bank policies can provide insights into potential interest rate changes, which can affect currency valuations.

Developing a personalized trading style.

Developing a personalized trading style is an important step towards becoming a successful forex trader. A trading style reflects your unique approach, preferences, and risk tolerance in the market. It encompasses various aspects, including timeframes, trading strategies, risk management techniques, and psychological factors. Here are some steps to help you develop a personalized trading style:

Self-Assessment: Begin by assessing your strengths, weaknesses, and personal preferences as a trader. Consider factors such as your available time for trading, risk tolerance, financial goals, and the level of emotional control you possess. Understanding your personality and trading preferences will help you align your trading style with your strengths.

Learn Different Trading Approaches: Familiarize yourself with various trading approaches, such as day trading, swing trading, trend following, or range trading. Each style has its own characteristics and timeframes. Explore different strategies, indicators, and chart patterns associated with each approach to see which resonate with you.

Demo Trading: Practice trading in a risk-free environment by using a demo account. This allows you to test different strategies and styles without risking real money. Use the demo account to experiment with various timeframes, indicators, and risk management techniques. Keep track of your trades, analyze the results, and assess which approaches suit you best.

Define Your Trading Goals: Determine your trading goals and objectives. Are you aiming for consistent profits, capital preservation, or long-term wealth accumulation? Clarify your goals, as they will guide your decision-making and help you choose the most suitable trading style.

Risk Management: Develop a risk management plan that aligns with your trading style and risk tolerance. Decide on factors such as position sizing, stop-loss levels, and risk-reward ratios. Implement risk management techniques that suit your personality and comfort level with risk.

Keep a Trading Journal: Maintain a trading journal to document your trades, strategies, and the reasoning behind your decisions. Analyze your trading journal periodically to identify patterns, strengths, and weaknesses. This will help you refine your trading style over time.

Adaptation and Continuous Learning: The markets are dynamic, so be prepared to adapt and evolve your trading style as needed. Continuously educate yourself through books, courses, webinars, and interactions with other traders. Stay updated on market news, economic events, and technological advancements that may impact your trading.

Patience and Discipline: Patience and discipline are crucial for success in trading. Stick to your trading plan, avoid impulsive decisions, and manage your emotions. Developing a disciplined approach to trading will help you stay focused and avoid unnecessary risks.

Remember, developing a personalized trading style takes time and experience. It's important to be flexible and open to adjusting your approach based on market conditions and personal growth. Regular self-assessment and continuous learning are essential components of refining and improving your trading style over time.

Trading Psychology and Mindset:

Overcoming fear and greed:

Overcoming fear and greed is a critical aspect of successful trading. Fear and greed are common emotions that can significantly impact trading decisions and lead to irrational behavior. Here are some strategies to help you manage and overcome these emotions:

Educate Yourself: Knowledge and understanding are powerful tools for managing fear and greed. Educate yourself about the forex market, trading strategies, risk management techniques, and the psychology of trading. The more you understand the market and the factors that drive price movements, the more confident and rational you will become in your decision-making.

Have a Trading Plan: Develop a well-defined trading plan that includes entry and exit criteria, risk management guidelines, and specific rules for each trade. When you have a clear plan in place, it becomes easier to stick to it and avoid impulsive decisions driven by fear or greed. Follow your plan consistently, regardless of short-term market fluctuations.

Practice Proper Risk Management: Implementing effective risk management techniques is crucial for managing fear and greed. Determine your risk tolerance and set appropriate position sizes, stop-loss levels, and take-profit targets for each trade. By controlling your risk exposure, you can alleviate fear and prevent greed-driven behaviors that may lead to excessive risk-taking.

Use Stop Loss Orders: Utilize stop loss orders to limit potential losses on each trade. Placing stop loss orders at strategic levels helps you exit losing trades before they result in substantial losses. This not only protects your capital but also reduces the fear of holding onto losing positions for too long.

Set Realistic Expectations: It's important to set realistic expectations about trading outcomes. Avoid chasing unrealistic profits or expecting every trade to be a winner. Recognize that losses are a natural part of trading, and focus on consistent profitability over the long term. By managing your expectations, you can minimize the impact of greed and the fear of missing out (FOMO).

Practice Emotional Detachment: Emotions can cloud judgment and lead to impulsive decisions. Strive for emotional detachment from your trades. Make decisions based on your trading plan and objective analysis rather than being driven by fear or greed. Avoid letting short-term market fluctuations or the opinions of others influence your decision-making process.

Use Visualization and Mindfulness Techniques: Practice visualization and mindfulness exercises to manage emotions during trading. Before entering a trade, visualize successful outcomes and envision yourself managing any potential losses calmly. Engaging in mindfulness techniques, such as deep breathing or meditation, can help you stay present and focused, reducing the influence of fear and greed.

Maintain a Trading Journal: Keep a trading journal to record your thoughts, emotions, and observations for each trade. Reviewing your journal can help you identify patterns and triggers for fear and greed. It also provides an opportunity for self-reflection and continuous improvement.

Developing patience and discipline.

Developing patience and discipline is crucial for long-term success in forex trading. These qualities help you stick to your trading plan, avoid impulsive decisions, and stay focused on your goals. Here are some strategies to help you develop and strengthen patience and discipline in your trading:

Define Your Trading Plan: A well-defined trading plan acts as a roadmap for your trading activities. It outlines your strategies, entry and exit criteria, risk management rules, and other important guidelines. By having a clear plan in place, you provide yourself with a structured framework that fosters patience and discipline.

Set Realistic Expectations: Understand that trading is not a get-rich-quick scheme. Set realistic expectations and avoid being overly influenced by short-term market fluctuations. Recognize that consistent profitability takes time and effort. Having realistic expectations reduces the temptation to take unnecessary risks driven by impatience or the desire for quick profits.

Follow Your Trading Plan: Once you have a trading plan, make a commitment to follow it consistently. Avoid deviating from your plan based on emotional impulses or external factors. Stick to your predefined entry and exit criteria, risk management guidelines, and position sizing rules. Discipline yourself to only take trades that meet the criteria outlined in your plan.

Practice Patience in Trade Selection: Exercise patience when selecting trades. Wait for high-quality setups that align with your trading strategy and have a positive risk-reward ratio. Avoid rushing into trades out of fear of missing out or impatience. Remember, not every market condition is suitable for trading, and it's better to wait for favorable opportunities.

Embrace Proper Risk Management: Implementing sound risk management techniques is essential for maintaining discipline. Determine your risk tolerance and set appropriate position sizes, stop-loss levels, and take-profit targets. Adhering to your risk management plan helps you avoid impulsive decisions driven by emotions and helps preserve capital.

Keep a Trading Journal: Maintain a trading journal to record your trades, thoughts, and emotions. Regularly review your journal to assess your adherence to your trading plan and identify areas for improvement. Reflecting on your past trades helps you become aware of any patterns of undisciplined behavior and reinforces the importance of discipline in your trading.

Practice Mindfulness and Emotional Control: Develop mindfulness techniques and emotional control to manage the psychological aspects of trading. Be aware of your emotions during trading and learn to detach from them. Practice techniques like deep breathing or taking breaks to regain composure during times of stress or excitement.

Continuous Learning and Self-Improvement: The process of developing patience and discipline is ongoing. Continuously educate yourself about trading strategies, market dynamics, and psychology. Engage in self-improvement activities, such as reading trading books, attending webinars, or joining trading communities to learn from experienced traders and gain insights into their disciplined approaches.

Managing emotions during trading.

Managing emotions during trading is essential for making rational decisions and avoiding impulsive actions that can negatively impact your trading results. Here are some strategies to help you effectively manage emotions during your trading activities:

Self-Awareness: Develop self-awareness to recognize and understand your emotions while trading. Be mindful of how emotions such as fear, greed, excitement, or frustration can influence your decision-making process. By being aware of your emotions, you can take steps to control and manage them.

Have a Trading Plan: A well-defined trading plan serves as a roadmap and helps remove emotional guesswork. Stick to your plan and follow your predefined entry and exit rules. Having a plan in place reduces the likelihood of making impulsive decisions driven by emotions.

Predefine Risk and Reward: Determine your risk tolerance and establish risk-reward ratios for each trade. This allows you to objectively evaluate potential trades based on their potential profitability and risk. By focusing on the risk-reward aspect, you can reduce emotional attachments to individual trades.

Utilize Stop Loss Orders: Place stop-loss orders when entering trades to automatically exit positions if they move against you. This helps limit potential losses and reduces the emotional stress of making manual exit decisions during volatile market conditions.

Practice Proper Risk Management: Implement effective risk management techniques, such as position sizing and setting appropriate stop-loss levels. By managing risk, you can alleviate anxiety and fear associated with potential losses and focus on the overall risk-reward balance.

Take Breaks and Maintain Balance: Trading can be mentally and emotionally demanding. Take regular breaks to clear your mind and recharge. Engage in activities outside of trading that bring you joy and help maintain a healthy work-life balance. Taking care of your overall well-being contributes to emotional stability during trading.

Avoid Overtrading: Overtrading can be a result of impulsive emotional reactions to market movements. Stick to your trading plan and be selective in the trades you take. Avoid chasing trades out of fear of missing out or making up for previous losses. Quality over quantity is key.

Practice Emotional Detachment: Emotions can cloud judgment and lead to irrational decisions. Practice emotional detachment by focusing on objective analysis and sticking to your trading plan. Avoid being swayed by short-term market fluctuations or the opinions of others. Trust your strategy and analysis.

Maintain Realistic Expectations: Understand that losses are part of trading, and not every trade will be a winner. Maintain realistic expectations and avoid chasing quick profits. Patience and discipline are key in managing expectations and emotions associated with potential gains or losses.

Learn from Mistakes: Mistakes and losses are valuable learning opportunities. Instead of dwelling on them, reflect on what went wrong and identify areas for improvement. Learning from mistakes helps you grow as a trader and reduces the emotional impact of setbacks.

Learning from losses and maintaining a positive mindset.

Learning from losses and maintaining a positive mindset are crucial aspects of improving as a trader and staying motivated during challenging times. Here are some strategies to help you effectively learn from losses and cultivate a positive mindset:

Embrace Losses as Learning Opportunities: Instead of viewing losses as failures, see them as opportunities for growth and learning. Analyze your losing trades to understand what went wrong, identify any patterns or mistakes, and gain insights into areas that need improvement. Use this knowledge to refine your trading strategy and enhance your decision-making process.

Keep a Trading Journal: Maintain a trading journal to record details of your trades, including the rationale behind your decisions, entry and exit points, and emotions experienced during the trade. Regularly review your journal to identify patterns, assess your strengths and weaknesses, and track your progress over time. This helps you learn from your losses and make adjustments to your approach.

Focus on Process, Not Outcome: Shift your focus from short-term results to the process of executing your trading plan effectively. Emphasize consistency in following your strategy, risk management, and disciplined decision-making. By concentrating on the process, you detach yourself from the emotional ups and downs of individual trades and maintain a more stable mindset.

Set Realistic Expectations: It's essential to have realistic expectations about trading outcomes. Understand that losses are a natural part of trading, and no trader has a perfect win rate. Recognize that consistent profitability takes time and experience. By having realistic expectations, you can avoid feeling discouraged or demotivated by individual losses.

Seek Feedback and Mentorship: Surround yourself with experienced traders or seek feedback from professionals. Engage in trading communities, forums, or mentorship programs where you can share experiences, gain insights, and learn from others' expertise. Having a support system helps you maintain perspective, learn from others' experiences, and stay motivated.

Practice Self-Care: Take care of your physical and mental well-being. Engage in activities that help reduce stress, such as exercise, meditation, or hobbies. Get sufficient rest and maintain a healthy lifestyle. When you take care of yourself, you enhance your ability to handle losses and maintain a positive mindset.

Practice Positive Self-Talk: Monitor your inner dialogue and consciously replace negative thoughts with positive ones. Develop a positive self-talk routine to encourage yourself, build confidence, and maintain motivation during challenging times. Affirmations and visualization techniques can be helpful in cultivating a positive mindset.

Celebrate Small Wins: Acknowledge and celebrate small wins along your trading journey. Recognize that progress is not always linear, and even small improvements are significant. Celebrating successes, no matter how small, helps maintain motivation and reinforces a positive mindset.

Continuous Learning and Adaptation: Stay curious and committed to continuous learning. Stay updated with market trends, trading strategies, and new developments in the field. Adapt and refine your approach based on new insights and experiences. A growth mindset keeps you engaged, resilient, and open to opportunities.

Stay Grateful and Practice Gratitude: Cultivate a sense of gratitude for the opportunities and experiences you have as a trader. Focus on the positives, such as the ability to learn, grow, and participate in the financial markets. Practicing gratitude helps shift your perspective and maintain a positive mindset even during challenging times.

Conclusion:

Congratulations! You have completed "Mastering the forex market: A comprehensive beginners course for financial success." Armed with the knowledge and skills gained from this book, you are now well-prepared to embark on your Forex trading journey. Remember, success in Forex trading comes with practice, patience, and a commitment to continuous learning. Stay disciplined, manage your risks effectively, and adapt to changing market conditions. May your future endeavors in the currency markets be filled with profitable trades and personal growth.

www.ingramcontent.com/pod-product-compliance
Lightning Source LLC
Chambersburg PA
CBHW080614220526
45466CB00010B/3347